Unbossed & Unapologetic

Poetry for the Awakened Woman

Tammarrah Addison, M.Ed., MA

Unbossed & Unapologetic .
Copyright © 2018 by Tammarrah Addison.

All rights reserved. Printed in the United States of America. No part of this book may be used or reproduced in any manner whatsoever without written permission except in the case of brief quotations embodied in critical articles and reviews. Permission granted on request.

Qui 2 Life Publishing
34 Shining Willow Way
LaPlata, MD 20646
www.qui2life.com
1 (301) 710-5219

Soft cover ISBN: 978-1-7326177-3-5
eBook ISBN: 978-1-7326177-2-8

Library of Congress Cataloging-in-Publication Data
Name: Tammarrah Addison
Title: Unbossed & Unapologetic

Edited by Tonitta Hopkins and T. Lynn Tate

Cover Design by SPJ Graphics

Qui 2 Life Publishing is not responsible for any content or determination of work. All information is solely considered as the point of view of the author.

I dedicate this book to my children: Trevion, Serenity, Brieanna and Grayson. God made you so resilient and I am thankful for that. May he continue to keep you in his grace and mercy.

Acknowledgments

I would like to first thank my family, my husband. Your unconditional love has made me stronger and more insightful as a mother and woman. My first team who believed in my vision of helping women to become Unbossed and Unapologetic: Sheline Ellis, Cassie Jordan, Kristine Barnes, Denise Henry, Carolyne Adkins and Wanda Bingham. The warmest thank you to my cousin Sheline. You answered the call and helped me develop my plan. Coach, I am forever on your team. Sheline, I love you girl.

Thanks to Little Zion Baptist Church of Smithfield, Virginia. Pastor and First Lady Blackwell you gave me my first platform to introduce the world to my voice, my spoken word. I especially want to acknowledge Melvin Blackwell, the young man with the beats. You took on the big responsibility of applying music to my words to create moments and magic. Mission Accomplished.

Thanks to all the people who helped me with my first book: my editor and publisher, T. Lynn Tate and her crew at Qui 2 Life Publishing. Shout out to those who helped market my events, merchandise, and brand my look. You are a part of my Dassle for life. So, remember: Don't ever be taken or mistaken for something that you are not. You call the shots.

Dramatically Yours,
Tammarrah

Contents

Dedication	iv
Acknowledgments	v
Part I: Superwoman	1
Stand Tall (Dazzle of Zebras)	2
Uncomfortable	7
Pioneer	11
Expression	18
Recognize (A Woman's Worth)	27
Wisdom	33
Organize	37
Mobilize	41
Aware	45
Name	52
Part II: Temerity	57
I Want That (It's Yours)	58
Mentality	63
Get Stirred Up	69
Inconvenience Fee	76
Temerity	82
Fathers	88
Be	93
Motherless Child	97
Black and White	102
Chosen	106
About The Author	110

Part I

"Superwoman"

Stand Tall (Dazzle of Zebras)

Every kid loves going to the zoo. We do not think of the fact that they are getting pleasure from caged animals. They are taken to the zoo where the exotics of the world are more accessible. It was on one of those trips that my daughter asked the question: Why are zebras caged? She said they seem so gentle and kind. I didn't know, so I looked up the reason. I found out that zebras, also known as dazzles, are a part of the horse family yet they cannot be domesticated.

They are strong-willed and stand together as a group. On a daily, in their homeland, they go to the watering hole facing danger, but they know they have their group support. So the answer to my daughter's question is that the zebras are caged because they cannot be broken. I told her that when you cannot break something you cage it. I had a realization at that moment. Zebras are a symbol and a testament to the strong will of Unbossed Unapologetic women.

She too recognizes her purpose and chooses to stand tall in the face of troubles and setbacks. She makes the choice to not let anyone or anything break her spirit. She depends on her dazzle, her community of like minds to be there at a time when she will go after her aspiration and she will need affirmation. She too would reciprocate their actions. She works on not allowing fear to hold her back from what is meant to be.

Becoming an Unbossed Unapologetic woman means getting a dazzle around you that will have your back. Your dazzle must share your drive and passion because you will need them to lift you up when you are down. They will be there to motivate you when you are restless and feel defeated. Believe me my sisters, this will happen and you need them there to say, "Yessss, Girl Yessss!" When you Stand Tall, it will be very beneficial to have a fantastic Dazzle around you. They will help you squelch your fears that are keeping you from your watering hole.

Dazzle of zebra, she who stands
As an individual,
Given the raw deal of being born.
From birth was scorned as a nettle rash
Lacking the qualities of the beard,
Pale skin and cash.
Told to bow the head or be discarded
Seen as being weakhearted
Because she was of lower class.

Just trash and the zebra stands
With words unspoken at the watering hole.
She knows that in order
For her to be heard seen freed
At one point someone
Had been on knees
Hanging from trees
Not given the chance
To get those degrees.

The zebra stands with words unspoken.
So in good taste
She goes to the backdoor
In poor taste
She is reduced to nothing more.
And now there is a distaste
Because in this case inequality, hate,
And the disregard of gender and race
Has been served
And it's cold at the water hole.

The zebra now stands
Facing the king of the jungle.
Been too afraid to drink,
To think to live.
Consisting of only blood
Sweat and tears
Not living, not giving
Not using the gifts
That had been bestowed on the soul.

For too long they allowed
A self-serving narrative
To be the declarative
That she, we are not worthy
To quench the thirst for life
Or be first
Dehydration at its worst.

She then calls upon the dazzle.
Knowing that a community with unity
Can bring down brutality
And give us back our humanity.
Knowing that finding your identity
And leaning on the trinity
Can bring back your temerity.
Knowing that fear being checked
Can bring back the respect
And put a new world order in effect.

I am here! I am woman! Hear my Roar!
I am here! I am woman! Hear my roar!
I am here! I am woman! Hear my Roar!

I spoke my truth, heard my voice.
I made a choice at the watering hole.
I would quench my thirst.
Being aware of my enemies,
Not giving in to the inferiority.
Fear no longer had a place.
I stood amongst the dazzle
And realized my stand
Had been the thing
That brought together the team.

I am a new soul
And never again will I
Let someone keep me from
My watering hole.

Uncomfortable

I have been told that pain is not a good thing. As we continue to live, everyone will experience it sometime in their lives. Why not make it work for you? You can find some light in the darkness. During these fragile moments in your life, you will want to quit and you might feel that you are alone. My friend, you may well be at that time. Yet, you have to understand.

Being uncomfortable is the time for you to grow into someone you would want to know. It is time for you to seek a new perspective or perhaps go in a new direction. If you have to go through trying times, you should gain something from it. Use your uncomfortableness as a superpower. It will build heart and stamina.

I have the power! SheMan!
I used to look upon being uncomfortable
As something bad but now
I know it is a superpower
That many have had.

Can't you imagine
Being able to withstand,
The heartache, loneliness and headaches.

Do you know what you have
Had at your disposal.
See, being uncomfortable
Gives you superpowers.
My women the world is ours.

See being uncomfortable makes you
Aware of who you are.
You won't settle
And let others meddle
At the start.

The nerve of them
To mistake your politeness
For a lack of strength
Especially when it comes to the heart.

Uncomfortableness makes us choose
And some don't like that
Because they hate to lose.

Choices have to be made
When you use your powers.

See do I give this man
Who hurts me attention
Or do I choose divine intervention
And seek him
Who can give me all I need?

Read in between the lines
That even crimes of the heart
Can't win.
Do I stay and let my dreams
Wither away
Or do I go
And become someone
I would want to know?

See when you use your superpowers
You have the art of persuasion
Over yourself.
You will halt the stagnation
Get in formation
And give yourself a standing ovation

Because nothing is more sexy
Than a woman
Who is comfortable being uncomfortable.
And ladies let me tell you some things
You might see
As you start to use your powers
And put them into action

And do not let them be a distraction.

See fears bring the tears.
As the droplets come please
Believe they are getting rid
Of the irritations we call
Perfection lack of direction shade,

Being afraid, comparisons, obstacles,
Arguments, low self-esteem, lack of
Dreams, let it flow,
Let it flow cause we don't want it no-mo
Your insecurities
See, your superpowers are on full display

The situation being,
You the first of your kind
To do something great
You will receive the hate.
You must be in the cocoon
To become that butterfly.

Love being in your messiness
Because when you come out
It will be with the freshness.
It is said that the comfort zone
Is a beautiful place
But nothing grows here if you don't try.

When the roses come up, everyone cheers
But when the weeds
Come everyone sneers.
You can't make everyone happy
But you can use your powers
To make choices and be you.
So be uncomfortable. Stay true.

Pioneer

Eve showed us how to do it. To turn the world upside down when we want what we want. Harriet Tubman showed us how to go underground to get things done. Rosa Parks' courage and selflessness demonstrated how powerful a woman can be when she makes up her mind. There have been countless women who have defied the odds to overcome biases, racism and unforeseen circumstances. These women have given us a blueprint to help us navigate through this male dominant world.

Their tenacity and willpower has not been without cost. Sacrifices were made, dreams were deferred and history was defined because a pioneer charted a course to make sure that every woman was not invisible but invincible to follow their dreams and have the same quality of life as the next man. These pioneers learned how to use their inner strength to be and do what needed to be done despite the consequences. They show everyone in their presence, within the sound of their voice, within the reach of their hands that they would not be taken or mistaken for something that they are not. They called the shots.

Pioneers proudly accept responsibility for their choices and actions. They see this as a great asset. There is power and great responsibility in being a pioneer. Sooner or later you will recognize that every woman is one and they need no artificial man made item to catapult her to this position. Pioneers use your powers. Go! Win!

Hypertension, Apprehension, in suspension
Now listen.
Are you paying attention?
I am going to take you back in time
And it may seem like another dimension.

A time where we were pioneers
And got through the pain with
Little or no tears.
A time of sun up and sundown
And the hours and days seem like years.
But we pushed through with our swing low
Sweet chariot, coming forth to
Carry me home.
Yet, now we trying to do it all alone.

Long before we had the pioneers
Stacking the bricks to create
A road of success.
No rest for those who are searching
For the power of freedom,
Who else is going to lead them?

Extraordinary times calls for
Exceptional people.
It calls for souls to go deeper
And crave that hunger for more
Channeling those who have come before
Who open the door, calling pioneers.
Calling pioneers with that

Sacagawea flavor.

She was traveling the roads, leading a man
With a two-month baby in hand.
Leading, guiding with her inner clock.
She was a pioneer with this leading
Thing on lock.
We women have the natural power to do What
needs to be done.
We don't need no cape, steel cover,
Or lasso.

See we are second to none.
Know your power.
But men, ha ha But men.
They are fascinated
With the gadgets that give them
Immortal control.
They want unnatural strength
And this can take a toll.
From Iron Man, to Antman, to Superman, To
Batman, to Spiderman I say be a Man. They all
searching for that agility.

But we women we have the capability.
Power beyond measure we treasure
The power of having a standard.
We have a banner that states:
We will not be taken nor mistaken
For something that we're not.
We call the shots and we are pioneers.
Unbossed. Unapologetic. You get it.

We summon up the leaders before

To light the way.
Sojourner you were a woman bold
Strong before your time.
I stand here today to let you know
I am going to let your light Shine.
Now ain't I a woman? Yes.
Ain't I a woman? Yes.
Ain't I a woman? Yes.

Harriet Tubman showed us
How to stop participating
In the master's plan.
We had already won.
You know she bad when
She didn't have to use a gun.

She was immune to fear blind to failure.
She had the shield of persistence.
Harriet Tubman the conductor
She was the first of the resistance.
Mothers of black boys
A commodity a rare breed.
History be told you were the ones
In the shadow who had to take the lead.
Watching the new whip reduce
Your black essence to flesh.

This chess game in which
You are the pawn
Will show your intellect
And put the question of
Who you are to rest.

Mothers of black boys you are

The conjunctions of the world,
Connectors, highly functional
And you are needed
So take care of yourself
Because you willed this success
There was no wishing

So mothers of black boys
The community stands with, and beside
You through and through. We believe
And honor you and your power to stand
And be that superwoman.
Women I am speaking to you.
Know your station.
Greatness is always in the moment
Of the decision.
I accept the fact that
No one can do it to me
And nobody can do it for me.

Don't complain for what you allow
Wow you create and promote
All events in your life.
So surround yourself with those
Who are manifesting at the level
You want to reach.

Expand your image of what is better
So you can teach
If it is going to be
It is going to be up to me.
You do have the power
And it is within.
Pioneers use your power!

Promote!
Win!

Expression

Express yourself! That's what everyone says, but once individuals start to do just that it becomes an issue. Someone gets offended because they don't understand what that person is doing, creating, or being. The question is does it really matter about what others think when it comes to expressing yourself? Sometimes, unfortunately, it does. Popular opinion can reduce one's expression to nothing in a tweet, post, or statement, if it comes from those in power. Expression should not be suppressed.

So regardless of the opposition, we must continue to press forward and use any available voices in order to help those whose voices have been muted or distorted. No one knows this better than women of color. Through years of attrition, women of color have pushed through and resisted the urge to answer to stereotypical rhetoric. Embedded in the mind of those who refuse to transition with time is a race of people who lack the intelligence to be more than a mammy or maid. Mainstream mediums have allowed harmful impressions of another race to be seen as less worthy of another, and this has hurt women of color deeply.

Therefore, it is time to speak out and debunk the stories that are harmful and malicious. It is time to tell herstory, your story, of how your silence and hers has allowed others to advance their destructive narrative about a race of people they don't understand, especially when it comes to their hair, culture voice, and style. It is time to tell herstory, your story of how your words and actions led to representation and the conversation that everyone gets to have a voice to express themselves. It is time to be open to another perspective.

It started with a hat.
A symbol of individualism
To loosen the grasp of master's hold.
Six days a week you toiled in the heat
Wearing the servant attire but on Sunday
You could aspire to be,
To do, to own yourself.

That day you wore your crown.
That way they knew you weren't
Messing around.
Clean as a whistle shiny as a new pin
Cool as a cucumber
You were about to get in it.
This crown personified you into everything That
was true.

A woman, you
With thoughts feelings and dreams.
A human being
Not here just to serve their purpose.
Purchased, yet you made it to this day
And had not been broken
That hat was your token.

You were amongst those
Who could run the race.
You were expressing yourself
And this hat, the testimony

Walking down the aisle
With your smile was the ceremony.

Many watch you strut your stuff
Because you had the guts to get up
And prove your worth.
These crowns of glory shouted see me
Because you had been in a world
That was demeaning
And put you on the sideline.
It didn't have the time.

But when you don that hat
You were a show stopper jaw dropper.
They would never miss you again
Because your crown made the statement
That you were somebody
And that was that.

Expressing you were a symbol
Of success just like the rest.
You had rubies and stones and feathers.
Beautiful and precious
You are ethereal with grace.
Through this ritual you were addressing Those
that you were waiting
To take your rightful place
As queens but the clock strike 12
It was all a dream.

Back to your reality of suppressing
Your expression because this ideology
Would later be seen as an oppression.
So now where can

A black woman express herself.

Maybe in the hair the act of pressing
Locking twisting perming burning.
I run my fingers through my hair
And I get that inspiration.
These strings was my communication
To the world these curls
Defined my existence.
Assistance to whether or not I get a career
First I had to adhere to the rules.

My hair once known for its beauty
Has been through a lot seen a lot of places.
My mind roams home kitchen
The place I really got to know
These tresses age 6 really found out what
Stress is
In the kitchen the place where you gather
For a feast but it doubles as a torturing
Chamber to say the least

Here we used the blue magic
To create black girl magic
But not without the tragic battle scars.
You smell the mixture of fear
Vanity, sanity but Auntie Johnnie Mae
Threat of letting you look like buckwheat
Make you stay in your seat.
This is why they say beauty hurts.

How can something so simple like your hair
Define whether you live or die.
So some of us choose the lye

To slick back years of mediocrity
To blend into a community
That was full of bureaucracy
That don't care for you.

Emotions overload peer pressure
Got you to have your hair
Soft and beautiful.
Jealousy says it just for me.
Self-esteem is yelling African pride
Because you're African best
With your dark and lovely self.

Yet, this multi-billion-dollar industry
Ran by others has grabbed your
Self-expression
By a noose because your hair mind and Pride
Is too weak and you are too busy
Having a conversation about whether or Not
these Remy curls are loose.

Wake up
Your expression is being dissipated.
Your hair its style underrated
But others are using it
Hair appropriation.
How can a black woman express herself in This
situation?

She speaks up. This causes a backlash
That even Kunta Kinte can feel.
She expresses herself through her voice
And says what is on her mind.
It's about time. Wait. The response

Why you so angry? You too loud.
I know it is ok to be black and proud

But. But what. All the questions
Subtle demands. Why you don't smile"
Why you haven't had a man in a while.
You ok? Is that really what you want to say.
Do you really want to come off that way?
What way? That way.

Man if you don't get out of my way.
She is trying to express herself
To those who still mop with dirty water.
Who still got Sapphire in their eyes.
Comparing you to the likes of Mammy,
Jezebel Esther anger fester.

Esther from Sanford and Son
With that fish eye fool mess
Did not show the black women
At their best she was not us
And we were not her
But that is what they saw
Imprinting forever in their minds
The phrase: Is you mad or nah.

Mammy from Gone with the Wind
Was given the voice of reason
But if she ever stood up
And expressed her true self
She would be charged with treason.
And in her own words:
It ain't fitting It ain't fitting
It's jest ain't fitting.. it ain't.

But Me and Jezebel can hang.
Wait. Stop judging. She was wrong
For being disobedient
And it caused her downfall.
But what if she would have used
Her intellect to help us all.

She was a mastermind before her time.
Knew the most effective aphrodisiac:
Expression of Power
Had uncandid freedom of fear.
She never cowered, ok with
Making mistakes
Rerouting her plans and
Was more deliberate
In her actions to get what she demands.

Going after what she desires was normalcy
Using her gift of sexuality a diplomacy.
She was able to recognize her faults.
She dreamed willed and acted
Wrong dream, wrong team but Nevertheless
She was not a quitter.

If only she would have had
The true one with her.
But GOD,
Has given you the vision
To express your thoughts, actions,
And dreams.
Do not allow the past to silence you
And take your expression downstream

In the gutter, flutter and float
Like a butterfly to what lies ahead

Do not tread lightly.
Always keeping that slight edge
Forge onward expressing with hats,
Hair, don't care.
Express yourself
This is why you are here.

Recognize (A Woman's Worth)

When you know your worth, it is difficult for someone to discount you. Worthiness for anyone comes from self-recognition first. Once you recognize that you matter, the thoughts and opinions of others become less important. Owning up to your special skills, faults and strength is essential for you to build up the confidence you need to take on the daily tasks of the world. Know yourself. Acknowledge that everyone has weaknesses. Knowing what will push you to the edge is key to keeping control of your feelings and the power over you.

Know thyself. If you show that you are unaware of your gifts that were bestowed on you, people will use your talents to create success for themselves. So take time to inventory yourself. What do you like about yourself? Can you capitalize on that aspect? Then do it.

What are you waiting on? What is it about you that makes your home, work, organization a better place? The answer is that you are priceless and you contribute. For some, you have to figure out what that is. Once you have had this come to Jesus talk with yourself, you will finally realize your worth. People will no longer ask your worth or doubt it because you and the rest of the world will finally realize that you are Priceless.

How is it you can tell me what looks great
And what is not.
I want to be me.
I love to see my body morph into
God's creation without your insecurities
Creeping into the crevices of my mind
Because you can't accept yourself
And the silhouette that looks back at you From behind.

You look and wish to see Batman
Yet you see the Joker looking again
Wishing for the turtle and see the hare.
I am looking for the right
And you see the wrong.
This whole situation is pretty ugly.
A woman's worth is not up to you.

I don't understand how you can make laws
To regulate my body.
You want to be the regulator.
Regulate this: images of women
Being abused
On public sites the trafficking
Of women and girls.
Where are their rights
Regulation on my tampons.
Where's the regulation on your trading Stocks and bonds.

It puzzles me that regulation on your body
Has been zero to none.
Listen it is not your job
To tell me my worth
But it is mine.
I proclaim I no longer stand in shame.
I come before you with a petition
Better yet a requisition informing you
Of something that is priceless.

This vagina has braved the intrusion
Of lackluster love and still went on
To birth a child who knew how to love.
This breast now low and limp
Gave nourishment.
This body provided the warmth
To a child and encouragement.
I am passion about me.

I have purpose, peace and power
And you man are in no position
To tell me my woman's worth
And I can shout it louder.
Just in case you didn't hear me.
I know my worth
And you need to be educated.

Recognize my worth a woman's worth.
You, I now stand up for girls
Around the world
Who are not allowed to feel
The empowerment of knowledge
This demolishes their advancement
And keeps the stronghold of apprehension

Tension of not knowing
What the future holds

Their creativity is stifled
Entrancement halted
Because Dick and Jane
Was never an option.
Know your worth
Know that you're continuing to strive
Towards excellence for your mind.

Persist resist those who tell you
That it is your place
To be in the kitchen.
Well then cook up your dreams
And stir in conviction
And serve them your greatness.

Persist resist those who tell you
A woman is better seen not heard.
I am going to slay
You then with this quiet storm.
Flash floods of insight
Will cloud my brain
During those moments of silence.
Which will brew peace, wisdom, power.

I will not conform
To your gust of wind.
Don't mess with me.
You know my ancestor
Eve with one bite
You know what she did.
Look it up kid.

Silence is my ally
Because he knows me best.

I will have my seat
At the table
You know the rest
And if not I will bring my own.
So recognize
As Nelson Mandela said
"Me playing small does not
Serve the world"
Who am I not to be great".

I will not give up
My birthright
For a bowl of soup.
I will not be duped.
I know my worth.
A woman's worth.

Wisdom

Superwomen as you speak, remember every syllable should be well thought out because words matter. When others hear you speak they know that you are the expert on the subject matter. The events and struggles you have faced have endowed you with the priceless information that will forever change the life of someone else because you can be a beacon for them, a voice of reason or solace. You are wise with wisdom. You are a superwoman. Continue to seek knowledge and be abreast of what is happening around you and in the world.

Know how things will affect you. You will have to let the people you care about know your interpretation of how the world works and help them. My superwomen they are depending on you. Your wisdom is priceless.

First going against the grain.
It can cause a lot of pain
Lots of other men may disagree
With this method
But sometimes you gotta do what
Works for you.

We don't always do the same things
But we can get the same results.
At first you may need to help
Because there may be some places
You can't reach.

It's ok to watch someone.
Ask questions.
Get the tricks of the trades.
Before long you will be
Doing it yourself.

Next, pick your tools carefully.
Some may be easy to use
And acquire and give you quick results.
The other ones can be difficult
To handle and take a long time
To master and be just as rewarding.

The great thing is
That you now have choices.
Fast and easy or slow and steady.

As you start to do this
Often you get better and better.
Most likely you will do this
For the rest of your life
So you will become an expert
And share your ideas.

You see son, what you have
Asked me to teach you
Has been known as a primal ritual
Into adulthood.
Knowing how to perform this tedious work
Is yet another momentous task
That will start to separate you
From the pack.

That childish look will be replaced
With a more mature facade.
As you look at yourself daily
You will start to see the man
You have become all because you asked.

I am proud of you that you taught yourself.
I can see the evidence of your bruises.
The frustration of someone pointing out
The mistakes even though they don't know
How far you have come.
We see your battle scars.
It is written all over your face.
You thought you were doing it right
Based on what you had seen.
Do they not see how you taught yourself
Do they not see
How you got over the cuts and bruises.

Did you see how you believed in yourself
As you literally took a blade to your face.
Not knowing whether or not
After the first stroke
You would bleed to death,
Or just have battle scars.
Thank goodness it is battle scars
Because every time you look at your face
You will see a warrior

My baby you will see a man.
You don't need me
To teach you how to shave.
Because in your asking
You just taught me
No matter what position I am in
As a woman I can still give wisdom.

Organize

Girlfriend, get it together. You know what you got to do. Who you need to see. It will not get done unless you make up your mind that it is important. When you organize, you start to prioritize what matters and recognize the elements that can impact your future. You will start to see what is helping you towards your goals and what is keeping you from reaching and achieving your objectives.

Getting organized means you have to assessed your strengths and weakness because these things will either help or hinder you. The goal is always to stay on track and fulfill one's passion. Organizing can be the lifeline to a better you and a bright future. Those who seek knowledge and personal enrichment will push themselves to organize the things in their lives because anything out of order can derail them from their passion and peace of mind. Some of the best advice has been to seek GOD first and then put a written plan into action. A plan without passion and a pursuit of excellence will get you no satisfaction. Get organized so you may have all your hearts desires.

I wanted change
So I became the catalyst
Utilizing the path of the
Underground railroad.
I am making tracks
For my dreams

You had put me on the auction block
But I myself had started
To take stock.
It amazed me that someone else
Knew my worth and not me.
Those people used my talents
For their own gain.

I wanted self-investment
So I was about to take that train.
I took Tubman's Temerity
And didn't wait for help to come
You see autopilot off.
Yet my very own wanted
To keep me in chains.
I think not.

Do they not know
The swamps, dogs, storms
I had to overcome.
Boy that's a shame
I have come from the low lying levels
In which any ordinary person

Would have failed.

I am getting organized.
You must remember
Freedom and living
Is for the bold.
On that journey I came
In contact with me
Trolled.

I knew first hand
Why caged birds sang.
You wanted freedom to rang
And your body is condemned
To hell on Earth.
Well then birth a revolution
That's the solution.

You get organized
I know I am
Not the only one.
I started with my thoughts
And put them to paper.
This choice seemingly
Gave me a voice.

Realizing that I have been told
That my body mind and life
Is not mine.
No we are not living
In slave days
It is a different time.
I conjure up the spirit
Of the activist to help me

Stand tall and rise
Above it all.

It has been stated
That poverty is bold
And ruthless and need nothing
To aid it.
Take this living to the fullest
Ravish it raid it.

Riches are timid and shy.
Court it love it get ambitious.
Campaign to it like a politician.
Slogan: Unbossed Unapologetic Superwoman.
Organize rising to the occasion
Of being the most authentic you.
Organizing to make your dreams come true.

Mobilize

You have to be a body in motion in order to get things done. Speaking about something is fine yet when you get up and start moving you will start to see how things quickly come together. The more you move and surround yourself around those who are movers and shakers, you will begin to align with their positive energy. My friend pray, put in the work and prepare. What are you waiting for. It's your time!

What are you waiting for?
I choked with the words
Getting caught in my throat.
I stated as boldly as possible
With the only answer plausible.
I don't know.
Maybe I am waiting for Godot

Trying to use humor
To mask the fear and shame
Because I just don't know.
I am losing hope.
I can tell you I say what I have waited on.
I have waited on the approval of others
To validate my womanhood.

Waiting on others to tell me where I stood
When I knew I took that issue lying down.
I've waited on you to complete me
So I could be happy and whole.

I have waited on the right time
To make that move
Because it was the right thing to do
And I didn't want to be too bold
Because it was the right thing to do.
Right?
I waited on you to love me
On you to love me.
Pulse check. Flatline.

It is time for you to realign.

You can't wait for others
To do what you need to do for yourself.
This isn't the status quo.
You waiting for others to love you
Has plateau.

I am my sister's keeper
And I tell you to mobilize.
Jump into the nearest phone booth
And emerge as you with your golden glow.
Cross your arms across your chest
And become the best power ranger.

Get into the know.
Become your own magnificent obsession.
Use positive aggression.
There is no room for angst
In this profession.
Prepare and pray promptly and profusely
Prevailing positions
Prevalent to your purpose.

You are an evolution
And what you desire
will come to the surface.
Everything that lies ahead now
Is an opportunity and has been worth it.

You are a unique offering to the world
Pearled inside.
Show them what is on your platter.
You is kind, you is smart you is important.

You matter.

Mobilize and say still I rise
With loyalty, intellect, this body check.
I ask again what are you waiting for.
This nagging for your purpose
Is not going away
And you going to respond someday.

Mobilize. Rise.
What are you waiting for.
It's your time.

Aware

What's your body count? How many people have felt your wrath because of damage done to you by others, or yourself? Are you going to acknowledge the casualties you have caused and the people you have taken down with hurt, yourself included? Think about it. On the outside you look put together playing the role; but on the inside you are damaged in pieces trying to get a grip on reality. You have been so hurt that you are guilty of rewriting other's stories interjecting yourself where morally you were not intended. You just wanted to ease your pain even if it was for a little while. You wanted to be wanted, loved. You pride yourself on being a strong woman yet inside dying because little do they know you are a widow maker. I am not talking about the spider who kills her mate after mating. You wouldn't do such things. I am using the term from firefighters. Trees that have prolonged stress are called widow makers.

This stress can be caused from a fire and from other trees. They are called widow makers because at any time they can just fall and kill anyone or anything without warning.

See, on the outside, the tree(you) look structurally sound; but on the inside, the roots (your heart and emotions) are weak and are just rotting. No one knows because you are so great at playing the role or looking strong and rooted. Until one day without warning you just snap or the tree just falls. Were there really no warning signs, or did you and the ones around you just ignore it? Regardless, there has to be accountability. You have to learn how to thrive in a dead situation and forgive yourself. Get rooted again and become a sprout... learning to live again in a new way. You do not have to be like Lot's wife looking back. Frozen. That was not the right decision chosen. It's time to become a rekindle soul... Thrive, despite of.

She smiles the best smile
While deep inside she knows
She kills them softly
Before it got to this point
She was told to fire her internal critic
Who was a cynic
And hire a cheering squad
Who would always stand to applaud

Yet in order for her to get to this
State of mind she needs to take
Some time and temporarily suspend
Her security for growth
She said never again
As she loathed the idea of being vulnerable
Not knowing that she involuntary enlisted
Herself in the demolition business

Taking down people's marriages
Passions That got in her path
It was a woman's wrath
The window maker deep inside dying
Crying for love wanting to just matter
Her weapon of mass destruction
Weight mentalities doubts burnouts
Stress regrets left her in tatters

See at an early age
At every critical stage
She was emotionally neglected

Rejected by those
Who were supposed to nourish her mind
Take the time and build the sprout
These lack of actions started the drought

Unequipped with the right tools
To give her steady ground
She started to plant her seeds around
Moving about like a wild animal
Her lack of control made her cold
Killing when trying to love
Her first victim herself

Scorched raw tired wounded
Consumed by self-hate
She takes what is not hers
He smiles, it drives her wild
Says the word hooked
She shook intoxicated by attention

She did the unmentionable
Broken covenant yet she gets
What she gets
And she thinks it is worth the risk
And she strikes again
Innocent bystander

The widow maker emerging
Surging to the surface
Looking good on the outside
She continued to smile
All while burning with anguish
But who could extinguish this yearning

She went to achieve degrees
Earning prestige
Outside all dressed up nice and pretty
But the inside compromised
Wondering how someone could hurt
The one they truly love

Burning the ties that bond
This was blessed from above
That Mary J and Method Man real love
It hurts stings burns
She is in a soap opera
As the world turns
She's tired of the lying
The heartbreak yelling
And she doesn't know how much
She can take cursing her existence

She was going to be the resistance
With that unbossed and unbought
Chisholm feeling.
She started reeling from relationship
To relationship tired unfulfilled
She moves forward with
Bulldozer precision
She didn't expect what would happen next
She looked at herself
Pure derision

Negotiation broke down
She could no longer take
What she had to offer
It was all used and abuse
With no self-respect

She has signs illuminating
From her aura of disdain and shame

She became a working billboard
She made sure people had it their way
Because what she was giving out
Was Mmm Mmm good
She loved to just do it
Yet she didn't know that
Soon she would snap crackle pop

She didn't know she was worth it
Because only she could
Prevent the forest fire within
Tim-ber
She wanted it to be the end
But God
Had her rising like the Phoenix

When others would have thought
She was down and out
Baptized by the fire
Underneath it all was a little sprout
Fresh divine like springtime
She's humbled
Looking through the lens
Of a rekindle soul

She wrote her Dear John letters
To take hold her direction
With a different perspective
She's moving on to something greater
No longer looking for validation
She had a realization that

Everyday in every moment
She gets to exercise choices
That will determine whether or not
She will become a great person

Living a great life
She doesn't have to be Lot's wife
Looking back frozen
That wasn't the right decision chosen
She's in a 12-step program
That on the daily
She will plant the seeds of love
Cultivated by self-worth
And harvest the national treasure
Which is herself

We know it is not where you started
But where you end
All our lives have been cut short
Because of sin
Sometimes it takes us crashing
And burning to get the yearning to change

Get estranged from being the widow maker
And stop burning
And dying from the inside
Know who you are
I am beautifully and wonderfully made
Become aware Thrive.

Name

To have a name bestowed upon you is one of the greatest gifts one can have. It is truly the start of one's journey to fulfill the prophecy of living up to what one is destined to be. In the Bible, Sarah was given a name and referred to by another. Sarah's name used to be Sarai. Sarai in Hebrew meant quarrelsome. God commanded that her name be changed to Sarah, which means princess, before she birthed her child. Her birth name would not suffice for the calling that God had put on her life. Sometimes God got to intervene and recreate some man-made things. Sarah was also referred to by the apostle Paul as Freewoman, a symbolic mother of the child of promise. This new moniker signified strength and courage. She took on these new callings as she lived her life.

Based on the bible, we can probably say she proudly lived up to those names regardless of her qualities of impatience and doubtfulness. When she was given names, it was only to uplift her hidden qualities. When she was referred to, it was to acknowledge the essence of her being a flawed woman who did not allow her mistakes to overshadow her strengths. She knew the power in a name, her name. Additionally, she knew that the names she would answer to could potentially give her power or shame. So I ask you, when people say your name, is it with great reverence? Do you answer to the name in which God has called you, or the names that people have called you that were generated by your mistakes or their misdirected hate? You do remember that you are beautifully and wonderfully made? Right?

Juliet, from the play "Romeo and Juliet", asked the thought-provoking question, what's in a name? She wants to know why it has to be so important and what does it really mean. You and I can answer that. Who you are is in your name. What you stand for and allow is in your name. My name is Tammarrah. My name means palm tree. I like to say I bend but I don't break because I have been through a lot of storms that should have taken me out. BUT GOD!

I know the power of names and callings, and I know GOD has a purpose for everyone's life. I don't allow anyone to give me a name that doesn't align to my purpose. I do not answer to names that try to dethrone me from my perch next to my God Almighty. Have I made mistakes? Yes, but I stand steadfast and still and will not be taken or mistaken for something that I am not. I already told you! My mistakes do not define me, better yet they refine me. It is a daily task to answer only to your greatness. I task you today my friends. Know the meaning behind your name and live up to GOD's calling. You are an Unbossed, Unapologetic Superwoman who will leave a legacy, and I am proud to know you. What's your name again?

My name is Superwoman.
I have been gifted with my hands
To create and mold products of the land.
I know that my name is my honor
In which I will be remembered
Like the 25th of December.
I am so super
That only one man on this Earth
Can give me what I am worth.
My name is Superwoman.

My name is Superwoman
I am not a female dog or a gardening tool.
I was sent on this to rule over animals
And work the lands
So why would I be other than.
Stop calling out my name
Other than what I am
Please get with the program.
I am Superwoman.

I am Superwoman.
I am wise and witty
When I speak I create
Testimonies that need no jury
My word is my bond
And I am aware of the impact.
Keeping my character
And name intact because
I am Superwoman.

My name is Superwoman
I provide and protect for mine.
Yes I am a ride and die
I am very cautious
About who I bring around my brood
Don't protrude on my tuff
Without permission
Being loyal and trustworthy
Is the price of admission
I am Superwoman.

My Name is Tammarrah
And I have Superpowers
S: for Standing Tall
U: for being Uncomfortable
P: for Pioneering
E: is for Expressing
R: for Recognizing my
powers and ability
W: Wisdom of those who
have come before me
O: able to Organize
M: to Mobilize
A: Aware
N: I know my Name.

I am a virtuous woman
Because I brought all the elements together
Unbossed. Unapologetic.
Superwoman,
That's Me

Part II

"Temerity"

I Want That! (It's Yours)

Whenever you heard the word "want" you probably can remember some adult telling you as a child that you can't have everything that you want. And because of this statement most of us believed it. So we have went through life settling for just the basics. We associated that word with being greedy. Well listen, just because you want something does not make you greedy.

Wants give you a purpose and you develop a drive or a plan to go after it. Did you know that wants can be defined as a need too? There are things in our lives that we need. These needs help us live OUR own satisfying life. It is perfectly alright for my wants or needs to be different than yours because we are different people with different experiences that will take us on different journeys. So today I debunk the negative connotations that comes with wanting something for yourself no matter how big or small.

I challenge you today to go after what you want. The constant drive to want things in life will keep you living and achieving. When you start to settle and come complacent with what life has given you, your needs and wants will go unanswered and your desires will slowly fade to the abyss. I know that was dramatic but so is your choice of not getting your wants fulfilled. Speak to yourself and tell yourself what you want. Tangible or not. You are now the adult and you get to rewrite the narrative about what you want. My friend, if you want it. It is yours! Go get it!

I want that!
That love that makes you feel
As if a thousand tummy tickles
Had been planted across your body
And you knew you were
Somebody's Shawdy.
That love that is unbreakable.
That pre Delila and Samson
Kind of love.
The one that can't be broken
For just a few tokens.

I want that! It's Yours.
I want love with understanding.
You know when you
Are in the eye of the storm
Broken trust, insufficient funds,
The heartache,
The feelings of wanting to run.
You feeling like you can't handle this.
Yet you want that kind of love
That smooths and calms everything
With a gentle kiss.

I want that! It's Yours.
I want that love
Where I don't have to compete.
You know that love where
I can be me.
Achieve great things

Without the haters.
Give my all to those I love
Without the traitors.
That love where I can be
Unbossed and unapologetic.
And those who love me,
Respect that and truly get it.

I want that! It's Yours.
So I want that kind of love
Where I am highly favored.
You know that love
Where you release the beast
Of self-doubt and
All you want to do is just shout.
That Ruth kind of highly favored love
Where you are adored.
You wait patiently
And you finally get yours and more.
Yessssss.

I want that! It's Yours.
I want that kind of love
Where I love myself.
That love where no matter the Circumstances I choose me.
That love where no man
Can make me feel ill,
Where I will keep it 100% real.
Where I chose God
To lead me hand and hand,
Where when it comes down
To losing who I am
I will take a stand.

I want that! It's Yours.
For those who try to stop you.
Tell them they are doing too much.
You're one person
They can never touch.
So tell them to take a seat,
Better yet take several.
You are now a rebel!
You already know
If you want it, it's Yours!

So keep turning over the boulders
Till you become shoulder to shoulder
With what is keeping you
From getting over.
My Superwomen
You are fit to do.
It is all about you
And now if you want it,
IT IS YOURS!

Mentality

Our way of thinking is so powerful. It is true that what we think can control how we react to the world. So if we think we are powerful, we will make choices that project these thoughts. The same goes for if we think we are weak. Our choices will reflect these thoughts and therefore impact our world and the people in it. The weakness of my mentality had to do with my love choices, my lack of love and the love that I had received.

I have gotten so caught up mentally on what love should look and feel like that I start to create a new universe around it. For me, my mentality, my way of thinking, was always about someone else. As I stated before, I was taught not to want for myself so I focused on giving others their needs. This cycle or way of thought depleted my worth and I began to not know who I was. To be transparent, my identity and mentality was wrapped into men.

I watched the female adult figures in my life, and I mimicked what I saw. I saw them disappear and emerge into shells of women whose only purpose was to serve men and neglect themselves. So, I focused on men getting their approval, love and touch. Fortunately, as I started to grow and expand my knowledge about the world and myself, and as I started to build a Dazzle of women who were comfortable with themselves and their choices, I began to look at life differently. I began to look at my way of thinking about myself, the people I interacted with and my view of love.

      I also focused on my mentality because I learned that I needed to protect my mind because it contributed to my overall health. Now, when I focus on my mentality. I no longer see MENtality. Men is no longer at the forefront of my life and thoughts. I no longer seek approval through them. I proudly see MEntality. I am learning to put ME first because I matter. I forgave myself for all that I had done because of my lack of direction, and I forgave others who did not supply what I needed as a growing child. Yes, our way of thinking(Mentality) is powerful, and we have the capability to change it.

Mentality - Approach.
Mentality - Mindset
Mentality - Attitude-
Men. Men. Men,
Have in actuality changed
My mentality
And the way I sometimes
see my reality.

But back to Mentality
Outlook Mentality - Temperament
Temper is what I get
When I think of anything
That starts with men
Because they got me
feeling some type of way.

The mendacities have me doubting
My worth and it feels
Like a mountain I can't climb or stomp,
Because I am asking for his love
Which he will not hand over willingly,
And it makes me wanna jump.

Because…. His mendaciousness
Got me wondering
Is he right for coming in
At 2 in the morning?
Hell naw!
Is he hanging out with SZA?

For the weekend
She and I got to talk.
If she and him
Gonna walk the walk.

I am out of my zone.
What must I do
To get you men-to-pause
Because we are tired of going
Through the changes.
Rearranging our mental state.
Escape - Is what we need from you
Is understanding.

Mentality is a way of thought-
You have me doubting
My own Mentalism
As if I am crazy.
Your infidelity…broken promises…
Lust for her…
We became the doubting Thomas's.

Mentality is a Point of View.
So after a long period of meditation
I asked myself if it was me.
Have I looked at the woman
In the mirror, no.
I wanted you so bad
That I became someone
I didn't know
To prove my worthiness.

Mentality a Frame of Mind
I am now a mendicant

Not looking for the typical
Bread and water
That will be supplied by the father.
I was looking for something
In my mentality
That I couldn't see.
Me

I didn't realize, or was it in disguise
That in mentality me came before men.
Yet I didn't see ME.
I saw Men first
And that led me to my hearse
Of broken hearts and untrusting feelings.
Limiting my focus
And I then became the locust
That swarmed on him
That showed me attention.

See Without Men
Me was mean
She didn't know her worth
Not allowing anyone else
To truly love her or enter her turf.
Me-was not a Member
Just a mess-Medusa-
you know the rest.

Me with her Mentality
Had no outlook, it was bleak
She reeked of no passion,
Low ambition.
She refused to listen to her heart
For it bled of loneliness and self-limitation.

It was like she was on a mission
To sabotage her unseen greatness

It was standing room only
for this show off.
Who would be chosen men or me?
We all know who it needs to be.
Yet- I beget to the heart
Because that is where it starts.

Mentality- State of mind.
Change your perspective
Of your Mentality
And it will improve the totality
Of your life-
You have to make a choice
Who will have your voice?

Get Stirred Up

Silence can be therapeutic and it can be deafening. We have, at one time, asked for it so we can clear our mind or have peace of mind. I have found myself asking for it. But when you are silent because of fear or hopelessness this takes this element to a whole new level. No one should be silent about atrocities or abuses that have happened to them. Yet, unfortunately, too many abused persons are. I want them, along with myself, to find the courage to speak up.

When do you say enough is enough? I say it is right now. Let's Get Stirred UP. Take that long step, say that first syllable and acknowledge that you are worthy to be heard. That you matter to yourself and others. That you are not a product of someone else's mistake. That you are here. Living.

Take back your power. Make this day one. Make the choice to put yourself first. Get Stirred up like your emotions. And when you have that fear of staying silent again step out on faith and remember this adage: Their insecurities and self- hate will no longer become our badge to carry, drag and display. We will use our voice because we have something to say. We are Stirred Up. We can't live or thrive when we have secrets that keep us silent.

I am Officially here to spill the tea.
I realized it had to be me.
No longer can I stand by and sigh
And allow the inequities
To happen to us.
Yeah, I am about to make a fuss.
It is time: To get stirred up!

Turn those negative thoughts
Into positive actions.
No more abuse
Denials, character defiles, excuse
It will be alright after a while child.

The flow of what you need to know
Has begun and after this lesson
It is mandated that you teach it
To your son, father, cousin, brother
Because it is no longer a need
To hurt a woman
Who was part of the creation.

Let's have this conversation.
It's time to get stirred up.
What's happening in the world
Should be crippling the moral fibers
Of our being.
Yet it seems it's ok
To treat a woman that way!

Abuse them while they're young and dumb
They won't have nothing to say
And they will just run.
The government has become the ATM
Giving abusers the platform
To silence more and more!
I say no more!
It's time to get stirred up.

Turn those negative thoughts
Into positive actions.
Silence is no longer an option
Because it has become a toxin
To our body, mind.

Children of the younger generation,
They will try to do a replication
Of what they saw
Snapping a girl's bra.
Smiling because if they have
Money or status
They know they will not be persecuted
By the criminal law.

How is that? This is surreal.
Can someone Kneel for us.
Bring to the 40-yard line
All the touches that were down
There unwanted.
Give a penalty to all the players
Who dance on our body
Even when the music of our voices
said No!

Illegal Contact!!
Get them out the game
This is a damn shame.
Call foul on all the bystanders
In the stand who did not give a hand
To those because of fear
of cheering for the wrong team
Retaliation.

Someone in this United Nations
Has to get stirred
And turn these negative thoughts
Into positive actions.
There is no satisfaction when we hurt.
I need you to get stirred up.

All those who have been abused.
The negative thoughts
Have been a ruse for too long.
Gone are days
Where you were told forget it.
There is nothing you can do.

No one knows the incident
The violation that took a part of you.
Made you hollow and left you voiceless,
Gave you fears and the only solace was Your tears.

Remember you have choices.
And we have the voices to get people
Stirred up about our singular situation
Yet collective journey that concerns
He, she, and they And when we are done

They will hear the words:
You have the right to an attorney.
Get stirred up.

Those who choose to violate and stand by.
We know longer give you a pass.
If you are not with us or for us
Then you are against us
And you can kiss our @$&%.
Your insecurities and self- hate
Will no longer become a badge
To carry, drag and display.

We will use our voice
Because we have something to say.
We are stirred up.
Don't touch us without permission!
Don't speak of my body parts
If you are not a physician.
Don't tell me how I should dress.
Defense Rest!
Don't come for me if I didn't call you---
Hashtag it is all about my value.
We are here for anyone who has been
Violated…
We are Getting Stirred up

Spilling the tea Giving
Life to those in the shadow
The Who's of Who, and the Me too's.
Get Stirred UP!
Take a part in this action…
Get satisfaction in knowing
You are a part of the solution

And helping to get rid of the problem.

We are here for that teamwork.
The Batman and Robin
Become a part of the political process.
Let's put what they stated to the test.
Get your voice heard.
Be one to make the change.
It is time for you,
Us to do the damn thang.

I want you all in the mix.
I need to see the most authentic you
Broken, healing, chilling, giving your all.
They saw the fall
But wait till they see the new you
Put together with faith, family, and favor
And the new glue.

You are now stirred up
And have broached the subject
Of never again staying silent
To the suffering of the soul.
It is a new feel but it's your new real.
Stay stirred up turn the negative thoughts
And deeds into action.
This is what we call a positive reaction.

Inconvenience Fee

I let a lot of people waste my time, waste my tears and because of this, I was wasting my life. Let me rephrase that: I allowed a lot of people to waste my time, waste my tears and because of this I let them waste my life. I allowed people in my life who were inconsiderate. I had a choice to make. Yes, it is about choices and it has always been about choices. I had to choose between them or me. I chose me.

I could no longer allow these people to keep hurting me or devalue me through their haphazard attempt of having me in their life. So, I had that talk with myself. Tammarrah this is your life. *(Your Name)* this is your life. We have to be accountable for it. I know we can't stop people from being who they are but as it has been stated we can control how we react. Through self-awareness, I no longer wanted to accept how some people treated me.

I set my boundaries. I knew how I wanted to be touched. I knew what I wanted to watch and listen to. I knew how I wanted to feel in a relationship and how I wanted to be treated. And I knew how I wanted to be approached and talked to. I gained so much temerity from just listening to myself. That woman's intuition is real along with my life experiences. I came to a point where those who choose to come into my life had to acknowledge my values and see spending time with me as priceless and as them living their best life with me!

A pop-star had this concept down. She knew her time was valuable and proceeded to charge those who wasted her energy and time with inconvenience fees. I loved that concept because I too am worth it. You too are worth it. If you roll with me and make the choice to hurt me, I will now charge an inconvenience fee. No, I don't think it is crazy. I actually think it is brilliant. With this clause being implemented, watch how people will treat you.

I don't even know where to start
Though I know I have to put
A price-tag on this heart.
What if I could really get a penny
For my thoughts.
Or a dime for every time
I heard a man say: It's not you it's me.

Dollars for when I hollered at
You for being a tease.
I can't let you take advantage of me.
You have to pay for this.
I charge you with neglect,
The suffering you gave to my soul,
withholding of the heart,
Wasted time and you hurting me….

There is a price to pay
It's called Inconvenience Fee.
I assess my situation
And say look what you made me do
With my hours, minutes.
You and I had an understanding-
Unspoken rule
That we would respect each other's display
of love and effort

Not realizing you were the Shepard
of broken hearts
I just didn't think it would be me.

Questions come to mind:
Why even waste my time?

That child from the broken home
That had the chance to get a romance
That she thought
Only Claire and Bill could acquire
You're -Cosby-Liar.
Then there were the conversations
the connections.

So you too think
The world would be a better place
If we would just love one another
I have two sisters. You, two brothers.
Our favorite place was at home
And our favorite show
Game of Thrones.

We were made for each other
And going to be in love forever.
I was assured that you
Would take on this endeavor
Of my heart with seriousness.
But It got to hard
You bailed...failed to uphold your word
Blurred the line between love and hate.
So for suffering of the soul
Withholding of the heart
Wasted time… hurting me….
You are charged an inconvenience fee.
Why did you waste my time
And give me pipe dreams.
I want back my support that I gave,

The tears I cried.

You are the boy who called wolf
You lied.
Why you look surprised?
I'm taking on the same motto
As Best Buy:
You have to pay for your play.
You must of thought this
Was Burger King
Because you like having it your way.

Naw I am more like Ford,
Solid as a Rock:
Because of your actions
I got to restock.
You going to give up something
For your inconsistency.
There were times you didn't read me right.

I am and forever will be priceless.
My time, my mind,
My thoughts are of value.
I gave them to you free.
I'm about to make my world great again.
Boo, there's an inconvenience fee

I am going to reclaim my time.
It will replenish my dreams fearlessness,
The confidence to say no,
The foresight to see a disconnection
Before your rejection.

See I have a choice

Or reaction to your gross negligent,
Carelessness and disregard.
Instead of letting you get away with Murder.
I charge an inconvenience fee.
And with that fee: You just lost me.

Temerity

Temerity. It is defined as excessive boldness, nerve, or audacity. You have it, and it is time that you show it. This quality will take you from Invisible to Invincible. Temerity contributes to one becoming an awaken woman. Don't let the fact that you are a female hinder your growth. Speak your truth.

You are a woman, beautiful, gifted and a child of GOD. It is power in being woman. The sixth sense you have has instilled in you the ability to pick up on nonsense from the male species. My physical and inner features allow me to attract those who will help me fulfill my purpose in life. Some of them will be really helpful and others will allow me to use my gift of discernment. Thank you LORD. We were born with gifts that would allow us to rule over animals and the land.

Yes, superwoman. In order for me to do all of these things I must also have Temerity. You must have Temerity. Many people will try to discredit me and my gifts. Destroy what I have dreamed and built. Try to say that you are stuck up or full of yourself. No! It is now time for a woman to stand and be proud of herself and what she has accomplished. Maintain your confidence. Maintain your temerity. Stay Bold and Beautiful, and maintain that temerity.

She's got to have it
Spike Lee was right.
If not, she would cease to exist.
See she was crafted by God.
She's not a snob
Yet she has elements
That make her walk just right,
talk just right
Be just like-Perfection.

Let me bring back to your recollection.
It has been stated
That you are the daughter
Of the most high:
So no one needs to be surprised
When you have the gall's balls
to say I deserve the best.

You are the G The Unbossed
Who moves in silence.
But it's a balance of being bold
And not too brass-
Then they say you have no class-

You don't make statements verbally:
Yet your actions reveal
you are taking over the world-hyperbole.

She bold, behold:
It's gonna be what it's gonna be:

And it's called **temerity**
And she's gotta have it.

She's gotta have it.
You must be that woman of agency.
Stop giving away your choices.
Put forth a cogent statement
Around the concourses
I am a real woman before thee.

Basic is not even in my vocabulary.
Remember you brought someone rapture
The day you were born.
A new beginning.
A woman capitalizing
on the woman in side.

She is not making picayune decisions
Because of someone else's lack of pride.
She's open, out spoken:
With the classiness:
It's called **Brassiness** and it's me.
What I got to have **is Temerity**
She's gotta have it.

Now you heard the statement
It's a man's world.
James Brown was making it clear.
That you as a woman
Would be second place here.
Ok, you can take that cogent statement
And make it an affliction.
Become the bag lady of the feminist cause
Till it becomes an addiction.

Trying to prove that a right was wrong,
And wrong was right
Girl we are women-
We can talk all night.
Instead, you know what you got.
You are the embodiment
Of the most beautiful entity.

It may be stated that it's a man's world
But you need to come in
Like let me see, let me see.
Tell them: Watch me do me.
See how these intellectual thoughts
Can do more than clean house.

Even when we give birth:
We are creating microcosms of
A new world
That deserves the know our worth…
Yet we tired of telling,
Yelling who we are.

Ask him: Don't you feel some type of way
When we compare you to
What we see in a jar
O righty then…
I think we are on the same page.

Being who you are is the new rage
So go get what is yours
I, she's gotta have it
Regardless of he:
And what it is, is Temerity.

We now know attaining these qualities
Can catapult one to success.
Yet, contrary to the belief
That you can make people do things
To get these and take the lead-
You can't make people do nothing.

You can't make people love who you are.
Love yourself.
You can't make people have things.
You can't make people keep
The main thing the main thing.
It has to do with the wiring of the mind.

But in time with the right dream,
A mastermind team,
Are you listening?
You gotta have it.
They gotta have it.
She's gotta have it.
My people,
Introducing…**Temerity.**

Fathers

I have uplifted the women in my life and around me through my poems and occupation. There have been so many that have impacted me in ways that I could never give them justice. I have also had some men- fathers who have showed me what compassion and love feels and looks like. My actual father was not in my life. The first time I remember meeting him was in prison, and the last time I spoke to him he was in prison. I knew he loved me, but he left a void that if it wasn't for my friends' fathers I would have never known what a real father's purpose is. Fortunately, there were men in my life even though he wasn't always there that showed me what a father figure represented.

These were men who took their role as the first male in a female life seriously. They knew that they were implanting the seeds of confidence and self-love for their daughters. Through their presence they are modeling the expectations of what excellence looks like in a father figure. The females learned and apply what good touches are, learnt how men talk and treat a person they love. Therefore, I want to take the time to acknowledge the men, fathers who love the women and girls in their lives. Ladies thank a man, father today. We love them forever and always even if we don't voice it. We love our fathers-Men who emotionally and physically take care of themselves and their families. Thank you, Fathers. This one is for you.

I believe they got it all wrong.
I'm talking about the hall of fame.
They only take the very best
In the field of what they do.
Then apparently, they haven't met you.

Fathers, we should petition
In terms they understand.
When it comes to hitting home runs
You are the Alex Rodriguez of the game.
You take care of home
Making sure every plate is filled.

The only strike we acknowledge
Is the one on the picket line
Where you are ensuring stability
And that everyone could live.

Fathers, you have been the quarterback
For your family for so long.
You've taken the hits of those
Who say you are not enough.
Regardless of them trying to sac you
You remain tough.
Choices had to be made.

Strikes, fouls, penalties.
But you didn't let this define thee.
You never lost your hunger

For taking care of yours.
It was given to you by the Lord.
Don't get it twisted
That you're not afraid to rumble.
You are forever humble.

Fathers, as one of the players on our team
you were all about equal opportunity.
You wouldn't let anyone out
Do us boy or girl.
You are our favorite guy, our world.

You taught us how to do it all.
From changing oil or fixing a flat
Or loving a person even if
They didn't love us back.
Your head was always in the game
Especially when you taught us how
To win in life, school, or on the court.

You were our support.
You were the first man
To show us sportsmanship:
AKA compassion and kindness
And that we should be heard.

And because of this
We deserve to be the MVP
In any person's life and they better
Treat us right
Or we're going to call our daddy.

Fathers, lets spill the tea on your tea off.

You have always been an Eagle
Spreading your wings to cover
Your family at no cost.
Even when the prognosis looked like bogey
You never let your family feel the loss
Of love, sleep no heat.

You are a hole in one.
Our prodigal son
Also known as daddy, pops,
Poppy, old man.
You know the rotation.
It's time fathers for your Standing Ovation.

So Fathers, today and forever
We want you to know that
You are our Friday night lights.
We never want you to be blindsided
By anyone making you feel
Like you are not an important
Part of our life. You are the truth
And we would not be here without you.

So today we petition to the hearts
Of those around that you be enrolled
In the fathers' hall of fame.
And as it has been stated before
You are not just a part of the team
You make the game!
Fathers.

BE

Be is to stand. You must stand for something or you know the saying that you will fall for anything. I say if you are going to stand for something. Stand for yourself because you are your best advocate. Be is a small word but has such meaning. Begin your journey of life so you don't settle. Behave as if whatever you desire is already yours. Speak it into existence (something positive) and believe. Be the power not the property.

My friend be the destiny and not the distraction. Put what you want into action. You cannot be passive about life and the choices that you make. My favorite line from this poem sums up what I really mean: To be means that you have to stop borrowing tomorrow's sorrow and sadness waiting on your Boaz or Ruth to bring you gladness settling for circumstances listening to the critique that create the weak mindset. Be who you want to be!

BE(Live)
One simple word that decides
If you live or die.
See you can either be
Or cease to exist.
So, you must make the choice
Take the risk.
To be free of mental bondage
To stop paying homage to death.
You have to….

Be-Aware that your thoughts
Have been bent and broken.
Compromised… taking you
On a locomotion
Of despair down the yellow brick road
That leads to know where
You have been tolerating the bae bae kids
Of your mind
Settling in the quicksand of your situation.
All because of your procrastination
So you must.

Be-gin to anchor yourself.
Realize that you have been acting Ridiculously
To not have life pay you what you're worth.
Make the happy times and money
Reign precipitously.
This will only happen
If you stop borrowing tomorrow's

Sorrow and sadness,
Waiting on your Boaz or Ruth
To bring you gladness.
Settling for circumstances
Listening to the critique
That create the weak mindset.
Getting distracted from your destiny
And not being who you need to.

Be-Come what GOD has made you.
You have the authority
You are no longer property.
You have convinced yourself
To not utilize your gifts
And that is robbery.
Be means you have the potential
The essentials to use
Your God given talents
Practice being practical.
Dream of being a dreamer.
Quit being a quitter.
Desire and drive will move you
Towards your purpose, mission
And you will transition to….

Be-lieve…like Loreal,
You are worth it.
No more mettling
In the depths of despair
Create a new forecast.
It is now raining down blessings.
We have clear skies
For what lies ahead
There is a 100 percent chance

That if you put work with action
You will not be misled to…
Be You. **Be** Great. **Be** Free!
BE!!!!!

Motherless Child

This world, our station in it, depending on the day, time or situation can make you feel like a motherless child, and make you treat others as if they are motherless. Without evening know it, we can take a blind eye on what is happening in the world opting to focus on our own needs leaving less fortunate people to fend for themselves even though we can help. We subconsciously detach, thinking that it does not affect us, but over time it can. This speaker spoke at a conference for educators. He spoke of a student in his school that was passed on from school to school, teacher to teacher and class to class. This student was the motherless child that no one wanted to deal with. The speaker himself was a scholar and everyone viewed him to be a well-mannered student who was going somewhere, and he got much support. Yet, the other student was someone else's problem.

No one took the time to help. He eventually aged out the school system, and with no guidance he went down the wrong path. The speaker however was very successful and went on to play in the NFL. The two met up years later but under dire circumstances. The speaker was being robbed by the student, and some of his family members were killed in the process. Reflecting on the situation, the speaker remembered this kid. He remembered how others as well as himself turned a blind eye to this student. How the student's problems were of no concern to him. Now years later, the neglect of this student had come to collect payment in the form of the speakers' family members.

"What if someone would have paid attention to the student the way they paid attention to me," he thought. The problems that the student had were never fixed, and they had now become the speaker's, who saw them years earlier, but thought it was no concern of his. What we think is a motherless child's problem may one day become ours if we choose to stand by. Take a stand and give a hand to a motherless child who ever that may be. If you choose to stand by, the unforeseen consequences can impact you for the rest of our life.

Sometimes I feel like a motherless child
Sometimes I feel like a motherless child
Sometimes I feel like a motherless child
A long way from home
A long long way from home.

This world has gotten to be hard.
Things that have been happening
Has been grappling at my heart.
The world, the people in it,
Is in need of direction.
Let me bring to your recollection
That there has been willful neglect,
No respect, and our moral compass
Has gone unchecked leaving some to feel
Like a motherless child.

The rationale is that the rank in file
Has our best interest in mind.
Yet I feel like they are inclined
To have me beg before they get to work.
This my people is our luck.
Noah Cyrus stated it best
We are sitting ducks
Leaving us to feel
Like a motherless child.

See I want to check
These feelings at the door.
And I know what a cliché.

I don't see any other way
I've been asked
To take out the emotions
And just give you the facts.
The facts are that these feelings I have,
Have had an impact.
My emotions are getting riled and
I feel like a motherless child.

I used to think I had time for things
But I am losing my patience.
Do you see what I see?
Do you hear what I hear?
It appears that someone has pulled
The wool over our eyes too many times.
Can someone get Olivia Pope in here?

This world is on the fritz.
In need of a gladiator
Someone needs to take out the spectators
Who are here to watch us crash and burn
Instead of taking turns
Improving someone else's circumstances.
I am getting side glances,
And I feel like a motherless child.
A long way from home
A long long way from home.
Sources say that our voices
Just got more powerful
Because of Google and Alexa.
They can speak for us.
But naw you got it all wrong.
They have mixed up songs
Of our heart too many times,

And we got frustrated
Because they didn't know
What we really stated.
And they are so overrated.

Remember when you were told
That everything that glitters is not gold.
Then you must be aware
That there is inaction, indecision, derision,
Lies, burning of ties .
There's brother against brother
And love and hate,

The undocumented state is a
Serious matter.
The government is in tatters.
Families losing their way
Because in 2016 someone made this
Our reality
This can't be the normality

But we mustn't lose hope
Cuz maybe it will be alright after awhile
But in the meantime I still feel
Like a motherless child.

Motherless Child Lyrics ~ Author Unknown

Black and White

Real love. I am searching for real love. Why can't women have it all? The job, the family, the love and the HAIR! Why do we have to apologize for wanting to feel the burning desires of love especially if it is what you want. Why do we have to stay down after a heartbreak? We don't have to.

Take love for what it is. Go on the journey and just like skittles taste the rainbow. Love can come in different flavors. Just like candy it can give you highs and lows. You have to go for the experience. I know it's hard to see things while you are in it but live and love. Teach your daughters how love should be and let them know that after a heartbreak they will survive.

We sometimes as women think we will not. At that state we become damaged goods. It doesn't have to be that way. Take what was good and learn. Go back out there and have your good GOD sanction fun! Don't be afraid to love again and again and again. Everything is not always as clear as we want it. Things in life is not always black and white.

He made her see colors.
She didn't know
It could feel this way.
As his glaze melted her heart like honey,
She was sweet for him
And stuck to his every word.
His moves and his kiss
gave her diabetes.

Just too sweet
And this queen bee saw yellow
A glow that would let her know
It was love
And she couldn't wait
For him to pollinate her mind again
Such sweet sin.

He made her see colors.
She didn't know
It could feel this way.
The sirens in her body went off.
911 was dispatched to her mind.
The situation was quickly assessed.

She was alarmed that he couldn't be hers.
Red with anger as the blood flowed
From every fiber that he could arouse
With just a look, a touch.
It was too much.
Is this lust?

He made her see colors.
She didn't know
It could feel this way.
Deep like the ocean blue
They were drowning
In tension couldn't breath.

Anchored down with the thoughts
Of them being parted
By the sea of circumstances
Choices… voiceless…
She was meant to be with you.
So blue.

He made her see colors.
She didn't know
She could feel this way.
He was given the green light
And he didn't make the move.
She became green with envy
Because the world gets to have him
And not her.

Things became a blur.
All the green in the world,
Would not change
The situation, the aching.
Still she called on St. Patrick
To see if a green four-leaf clover
Would make them lovers.
Superstition failed.

He made her see colors.

She didn't know she could feel this way.
Now she knows
Things are not just
Black and white.

Chosen

It is an honor to be picked. To have someone say to you I want you. That you have something of value that can be used. That you are part of a selection or a pedigree that is unmatched. You do know that I am talking about you. Yes, the one who is reading this. Some people did not make it to this point so I am so proud of you. You say, what have I done. Girl, you are still in the race.

You are not allowing anyone to take your shine or glory. And you have accepted the challenge of whatever is before you. Therefore, I leave you with a quote from a friend, Victoria Riollano. She stated it best that when you are chosen all these things happen:

> You go from broken to beautiful
> From defeated to a conqueror
> From worn down to a worshipper
> From afraid to brave
> From lost to saved
> From rejected to accepted
> From confused to full of trust
> My friend, go forth into your glory….
> You are the CHOSEN ONE!

You, yes you are chosen.
Have you Rosen to the occasion.
To be you through and through.
Warts and all,
Standing Tall.
No backs against the wall.

Your purpose has been revealed
The reason why you're here,
You were chosen.
Yes, you with the perception
That life is tough.
You've had it rough.

No one knows the personal battles
of depression, aggression
the hard knock lessons
you had to endure.
Being unsure if life is worth it.
Yes, my friend it is.
That is why you live.

You are chosen to slay
Your Goliath daily
And the battle scars are a sign
That you made it.
You are a worthy opponent
Because you never gave up.
It is not luck.

You are chosen.

We look at the courage
Of how you don't allow
Life's mountains to swallow you whole.
Being in the belly of despair
Questioning why you are here.
Yet, we see you Chosen One
Fighting the elements of destruction
Allowing no raucous to get in the way
Of your greatness.

You are our Rocky Balboa
Our Mike without the ear bite.
You are hearing us chant.
Fight! Fight! Fight!
Against the tears,
The naysayers, the dream slayers,
The monsters under the bed.
Do not be misled.

None of this can keep you
From your destiny.
Because when you look in the mirror
You will see,
The chosen one, thee.
I know being chosen
Is not always great.
There will be mistakes
Casualties, the reluctant one
Who chooses to run.
But at the end
You will be in the same place.
You have to be in the race.
So believe that you
Have a purpose.

It is your time to work it.
That every problem
will have a solution
And if not you the chosen one
Will start a revolution.

The battle scars are
A beautification status
To show that you are the baddest.
So remember you have Superpowers
You are the chosen one
The battle is already won.

About The Author

Tammarrah Addison, M.Ed., MA, is an educator, creativity coach, and poetess. She earned a Bachelor of Theatre Arts from San Diego State University, a Masters of Education from Azusa Pacific University, and a Masters of Theatre Education from Regent University. She is a certified theatre and speech teacher who has directed over 20 shows on both coasts as well as in Japan. In 2018, she became a certified teaching artist for the Virginia Commission of the Arts.

In 2017 she released her first spoken word album called "Unbossed Unapologetic Vol 1: Superwoman". It provides women with 10 Power Boosters that will help make them super successful in their daily journey called life. Her new album "Unbossed Unapologetic Vol 2: TEMERITY," which came out in July 2018, provides women with more tools to strive and fight for their desires and needs.

Tammarrah's mission is to help young girls and women position themselves to be the most Unbossed Unapologetic Superwomen they can be. Remember: Don't ever be mistaken or taken for something that you are not! You call the shot.